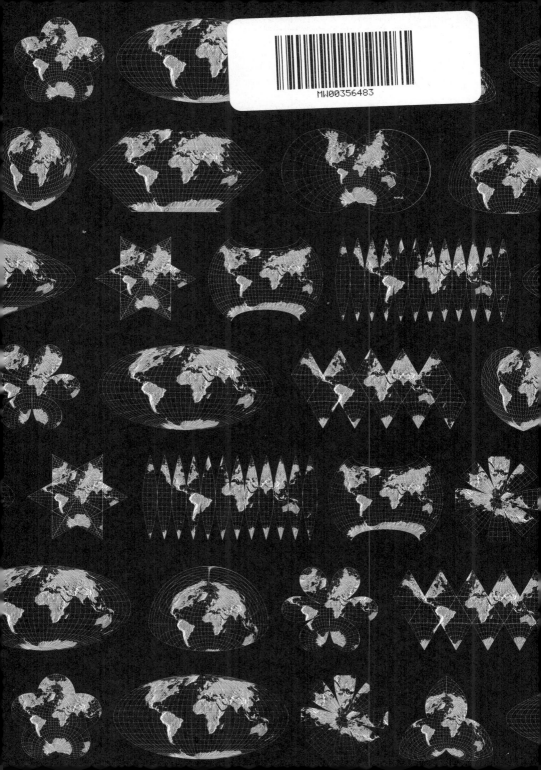

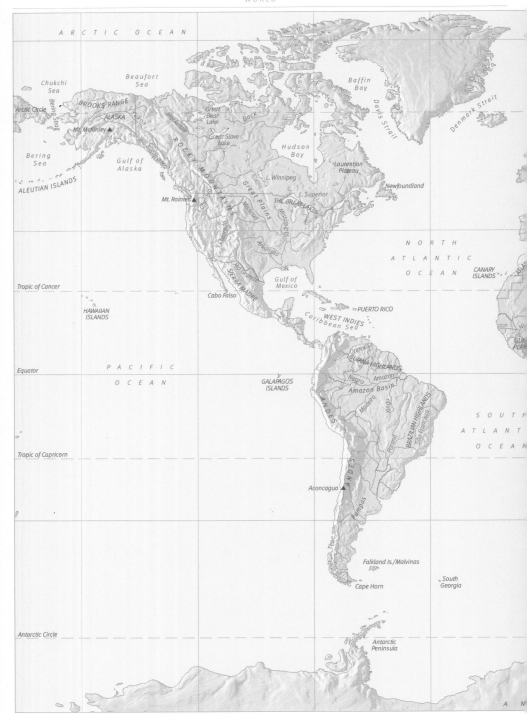

ARCTIC OCEAN

Chukchi
Sea

Beaufort
Sea

Baffin
Bay

Arctic Circle

Bering Strait

BROOKS RANGE

ALASKA

Mt. McKinley ▲

Yukon

Mackenzie

Great
Bear
Lake

Back

Great Slave
Lake

Davis Strait

Denmark Strait

Bering
Sea

Gulf of
Alaska

R O C K Y   M O U N T A I N S

Hudson
Bay

Laurentian
Plateau

ALEUTIAN ISLANDS

Mt. Rainier ▲

Columbia

L. Winnipeg

Great Plains

Missouri

L. Superior

THE GREAT LAKES

Newfoundland

NORTH

ATLANTIC

OCEAN

Colorado

Arkansas

Mississippi

CANARY
ISLANDS

Tropic of Cancer

SIERRA MADRE

RIO GRANDE

Gulf of
Mexico

Cabo Falso

PUERTO RICO

WEST INDIES
Caribbean Sea

HAWAIIAN
ISLANDS

GUI
PLA

Equator

PACIFIC

OCEAN

GALAPAGOS
ISLANDS

Orinoco

GUIANA HIGHLANDS

Negro

Amazon

Amazon Basin

ANDES

Madeira

Xingu

BRAZILIAN HIGHLANDS

São Francisco

SOUTH

ATLANT

OCEA

Tropic of Capricorn

Paraná

Paraguay

Aconcagua ▲

ANDES

Pampas

The Andes

Falkland Is./Malvinas

South
Georgia

Cape Horn

Antarctic Circle

Antarctic
Peninsula

A   N

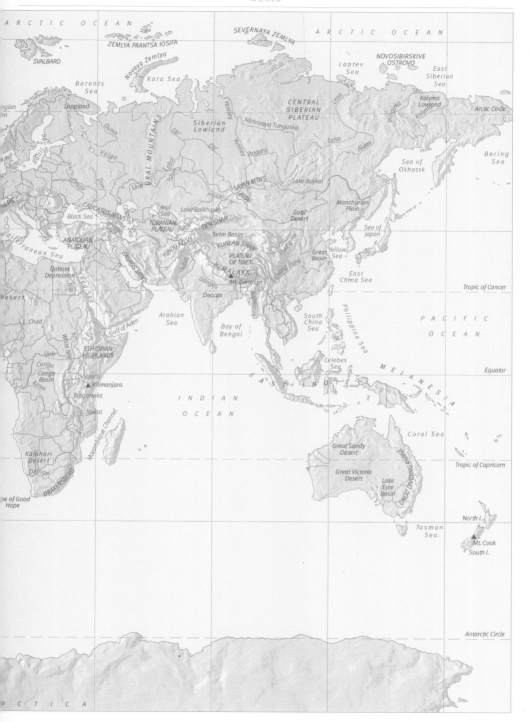

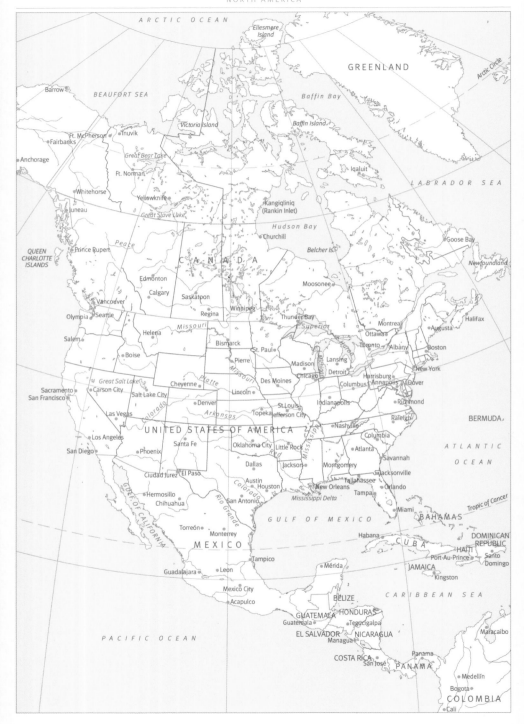

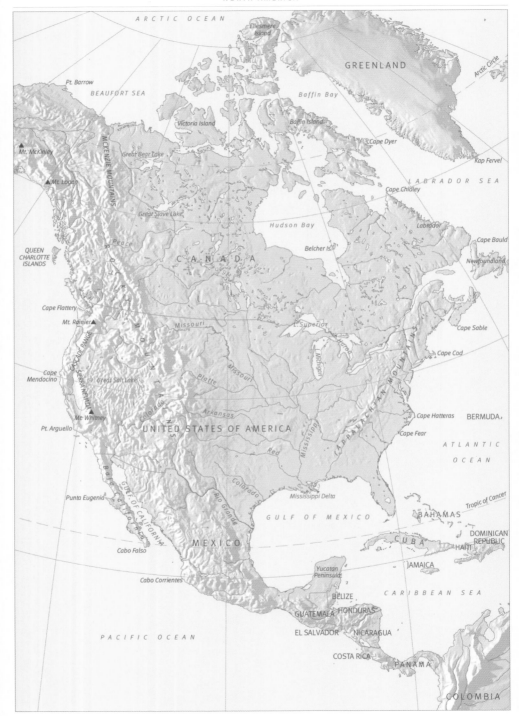

ARCTIC OCEAN

Ellesmere
Island

GREENLAND

Pt. Barrow

BEAUFORT SEA

Baffin Bay

Arctic Circle

Victoria Island

Baffin Island

Mt. McKinley

Great Bear Lake

Cape Dyer

Kap Fervel

Mt. Logan

MCKENZIE MOUNTAINS

LABRADOR SEA

Great Slave Lake

Cape Chidley

Labrador

QUEEN
CHARLOTTE
ISLANDS

Peace

C A N A D A

Hudson Bay

Belcher Is.

Cape Bauld

Newfoundland

Cape Flattery

Mt. Rainier▲

Missouri

L. Superior

Cape Sable

Cape
Mendocino

CASCADE RANGE

SIERRA NEVADA

Great Salt Lake

Colorado

Platte

Missouri

Michigan

Cape Cod

Mt. Whitney▲

Arkansas

APPALACHIAN MOUNTAINS

Pt. Arguello

UNITED STATES OF AMERICA

Red

Mississippi

Cape Hatteras

BERMUDA

Cape Fear

ATLANTIC

OCEAN

Colorado

Punta Eugenia

Rio Grande

Mississippi Delta

Tropic of Cancer

GULF OF MEXICO

BAHAMAS

Cabo Falso

GULF OF CALIFORNIA

Baja California

MEXICO

CUBA

DOMINICAN
REPUBLIC

HAITI

JAMAICA

Cabo Corrientes

Yucatan
Peninsula

CARIBBEAN SEA

PACIFIC OCEAN

BELIZE

GUATEMALA

HONDURAS

EL SALVADOR

NICARAGUA

COSTA RICA

PANAMA

COLOMBIA

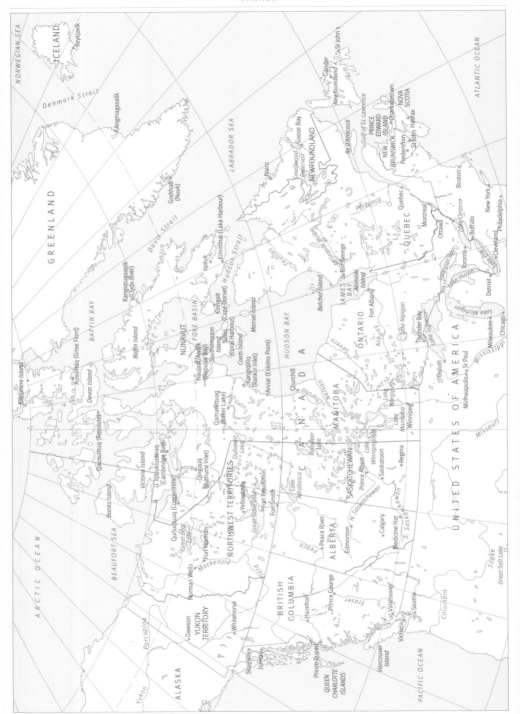

GULF OF
ST. LAWRENCE

Prince Edward
Island

yden

Lake
Nipigon

C A N A D A

Timmins

Kirkland lake

Quebec

Halifax

St. John

Nova Scotia

Thunder Bay

Sudbury

MAINE

Bangor

Lake Superior

Sault Ste. Marie

Georgian Bay

Montreal

Ottawa

Burlington

Augusta

Duluth

Marquette

Lake Huron

Montpelier

Portland

VERMONT

WISCONSIN

St Paul
polis

Eau Claire

Green Bay

MICHIGAN

Kingston

Toronto

Lake Ontario

NEW
YORK

Syracuse

NEW
HAMPSHIRE

Concord

MASSACHUSETTS

Boston

La Crosse

Grand Rapids

Hamilton

Rochester

Albany

Hartford

Providence

RHODE ISLAND

Milwaukee

Lansing

London

Buffalo

CONNECTICUT

Madison

Cedar Rapids

Rockford

Detroit

Windsor

Lake Erie

Erie

Scranton

NEW
JERSEY

New York

Moines

Chicago

Gary

Cleveland

PENNSYLVANIA

Philadelphia

Trenton

IOWA

Davenport

Toledo

Akron

Harrisburg

Wilmington

Peoria

OHIO

Pittsburgh

Baltimore

Dover

DELAWARE

ILLINOIS

INDIANA

Columbus

Dayton

WASHINGTON D.C.

Annapolis

Delaware Bay

MARYLAND

Springfield

Indianapolis

Cincinnati

WEST
VIRGINIA

Richmond

Jefferson
City

Louisville

Frankfort

Charleston

Ohio

VIRGINIA

Chesapeake Bay

as City

St Louis

Evansville

Lexington

Roanoke

Norfolk

MISSOURI

Paducah

KENTUCKY

Greensboro

Raleigh

lin

Springfield

Nashville

Knoxville

Winston-Salem

NORTH
CAROLINA

ARKANSAS

Memphis

Chattanooga

TENNESSEE

Tennessee

Charlotte

Greenville

SOUTH
CAROLINA

Wilmington

Smith

Arkansas

Columbia

Little Rock

Atlanta

Augusta

Charleston

ATLANTIC OCEAN

exarkana

Greenville

Birmingham

Macon

Savannah

MISSISSIPPI

Meridian

ALABAMA

Columbus

GEORGIA

Shreveport

Jackson

Montgomery

Albany

LOUISIANA

Mississippi

Alexandria

Tallahassee

Jacksonville

St. Augustine

Baton Rouge

Mobile

Pensacola

Daytona Beach

Beaumont

New Orleans

FLORIDA

Port Arthur

Orlando

alveston

Mississippi Delta

Tampa

Grand
Bahama
Island

BAHAMAS

St. Petersburg

West Palm Beach

GULF OF MEXICO

Lake
Okeechobee

Fort Myers

Miami

Nassau

Andros
Island

Tropic of Cancer

TURKS & CAICOS
ISLANDS

Key West

Florida Keys

Straits of Florida

Metanzas

Great Inagua
Island

Havana

Santa Clara

Pinar del Rio

Cienfuegos

CUBA

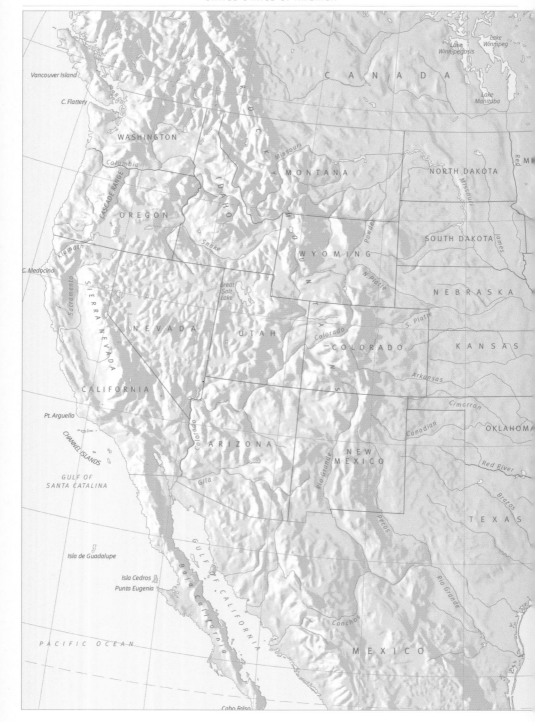

Vancouver Island

C. Flattery

WASHINGTON

Columbia

CASCADE RANGE

OREGON

Klamath

C. Mendocino

Sacramento

SIERRA NEVADA

NEVADA

CALIFORNIA

Pt. Arguello

CHANNEL ISLANDS

GULF OF
SANTA CATALINA

Isla de Guadalupe

Isla Cedros
Punta Eugenia

PACIFIC OCEAN

GULF OF CALIFORNIA

Baja California

Cabo Falso

Colorado

Gila

ARIZONA

UTAH

Great
Salt
Lake

Snake

IDAHO

ROCKY

Missouri

MONTANA

WYOMING

Powder

N. Platte

Colorado

COLORADO

MOUNTAINS

S. Platte

Arkansas

NEW
MEXICO

Rio Grande

Pecos

Conchos

MEXICO

Rio Grande

CANADA

Lake
Winnipeg

Lake
Winnipegosis

Lake
Manitaba

Red

M

NORTH DAKOTA

Missouri

SOUTH DAKOTA

James

NEBRASKA

KANSAS

Cimarron

Canadian

OKLAHOMA

Red River

Brazos

TEXAS

GULF OF
ST. LAWRENCE

Prince Edward
Island

CANADA

Lake
Nipigon

Nova Scotia

MAINE

Cape Sable

Lake Superior

VERMONT

NEW
HAMPSHIRE

Georgian Bay

Lake Huron

WISCONSIN

NEW
YORK

MASSACHUSETTS

Cape Cod

Lake Ontario

MICHIGAN

RHODE ISLAND
CONNECTICUT

Mississippi

Lake Michigan

Lake Erie

PENNSYLVANIA

NEW
JERSEY

OWA

OHIO

Delaware Bay

DELAWARE

ILLINOIS

INDIANA

WASHINGTON D.C.

MARYLAND

WEST
VIRGINIA

Ohio

VIRGINIA

Chesapeake Bay

ISSOURI

KENTUCKY

Cape Hatteras

NORTH
CAROLINA

RKANSAS

TENNESSEE

Arkansas

APPALACHIAN MOUNTAINS

SOUTH
CAROLINA

Cape Fear

Tennessee

Alabama

ALABAMA

ATLANTIC OCEAN

MISSISSIPPI

GEORGIA

LOUISIANA

Mississippi

FLORIDA

Cape Canaveral

Grand
Bahama
Island

Mississippi Delta

BAHAMAS

Lake
Okeechobee

Tropic of Cancer

GULF OF MEXICO

Andros
Island

TURKS & CAICOS
ISLANDS

Florida Keys

Great Inagua
Island

Straits of Florida

CUBA

CARIBBEAN SEA
Gulf of Venezuela
LESSER ANTILLES
TRINIDAD & TOBAGO
ATLANTIC OCEAN
PANAMA
Gulf of Panama
Lake Maracaibo
Orinoco
Delta del Orinoco
Cabo Corrientes
VENEZUELA
GUYANA
FRENCH GUIANA
Punta Galera
COLOMBIA
GUIANA HIGHLANDS
SURINAM
Magdalena
Orinoco
ECUADOR
Branco
Equator
Amazon
B. de Marajó
I. de Marajó
B. de São Marcos
Putumayo
Japurá
Negro
Tocantins
Marañón
SELVAS
Cabo de São Roque
Punta Aguja
Juruá
Madeira
Tapajós
Xingu
CAATINGAS
Purus
Araguaia
Lago de Sobradinho
Parnaíba
São Francisco
PERU
SIERRA DOS PARECIS
BRAZIL
Lake Titicaca
Arinos
PLANALTO DE MATO GROSSO
Guaporé
BRAZILIAN HIGHLANDS
Mamoré
BOLIVIA
Lake Poopó
ALTIPLANO
CAMPOS
ATACAMA DESERT
GRAN CHACO
ANDES MOUNTAINS
Paraná
Reprisa Ilha Grande
PARAGUAY
Pilcomayo
Lago Itaipú
Cabo de São Tomé
CHILE
Salado
SERRA DO MAR
Cabo Frio
Tropic of Capricorn
PACIFIC OCEAN
Mar Chiquita
Uruguay
ATLANTIC OCEAN
ARGENTINA
Lagôa dos Patos
URUGUAY
Lagôa Mirim
Salado
PAMPAS
Rio de La Plata
Cabo San Antonio
Colorado
Negro
Bahía Blanca
Golfo San Matias
Pena. Valdés
Isla de Chiloé
Chubut
ARCHIPELAGO DE LOS CHONOS
Golfo de San Jorge
C. Tres Puntas
FALKLAND/MALVINAS ISLANDS
Bahía Grande
West Falkland
East Falkland
ARCHIPELAGO REINA ADELAIDE
Strait of Magellan
Tierra del Fuego
C. San Diego
Cape Horn
SCOTIA SEA
South Georgia

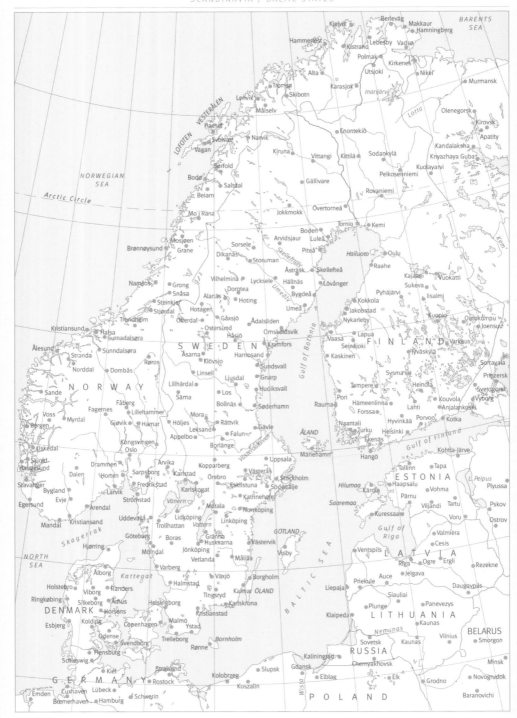

SHETLAND
ISLANDS

Foula

Fair Isle

NORTH
SEA

ORKNEY
ISLANDS

Cape
Wrath

Butt of Lewis

North Minch

OUTER
HEBRIDES

Lewis

St. Kilda

North Uist

Skye

South Uist

Ness

Spey

Don

Barra

Rum

Dee

Coll

GRAMPIAN MTS.

Tiree

Mull

SCOTLAND

ATLANTIC
OCEAN

Moray Firth

Firth of Forth

Islay

Forth

Clyde

Firth of Forth

Arran

Nith

Tweed

Holy I.

NORTH
CHANNEL

CHEVIOT HILLS

Malin Head

Tory I.

Rathlin I.

Aran I.

SPERRIN
MTS

Tyne

Lake
District

NORTHERN IRELAND

Lower
Lough
Erne

Lough
Neagh

P
E
N
N
I
N
E
S

Donegal Bay

SLIEVE
GAMPH

Upper
Lough
Erne

Lough
Allen

Isle of Man

Flamborough Head

Achill Head

Lough
Conn

Walney I.

Swale

Lough
Mask

Lough
Ree

IRISH
SEA

Spurn Head

Lough
Corrib

Galway Bay

IRELAND

Liffey

Shannon

Lough Derg

BOG OF
ALLEN

WICKLOW
MTS.

Caernarfon
Bay

Trent

ENGLAND

The
Wash

ARAN ISLANDS

Wicklow
Head

Welland

Loop Head

Cardigan
Bay

Dingle Bay

GALTY MTS.

Greenore
Point

WALES

Wye

Severn

COTSWOLD HILLS

Hook
Head

Mizen Head

Old Head of Kinsale

ST. GEORGES CHANNEL

Thames

NORTH DOWNS

Lundy

Bristol Channel

SOUTH DOWNS

DARTMOOR

Portland Bill

Isle of Wight

ENGLISH CHANNEL

Lyme Bay

ISLES OF
SCILLY

Alderney

CHANNEL
ISLANDS

Guernsey

Jersey

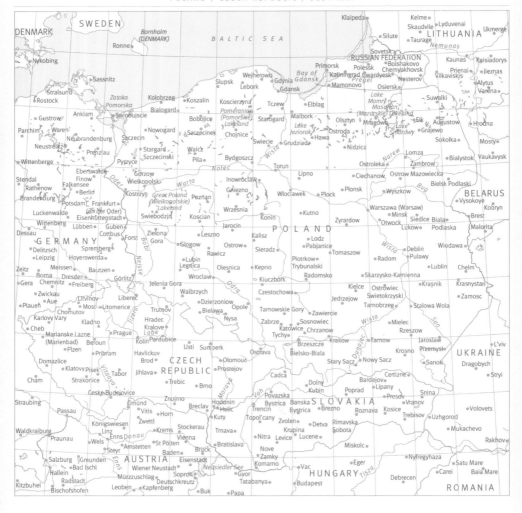

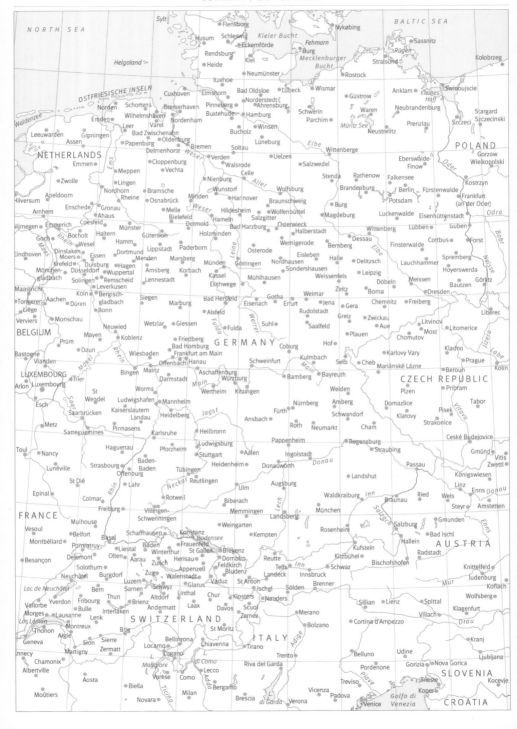

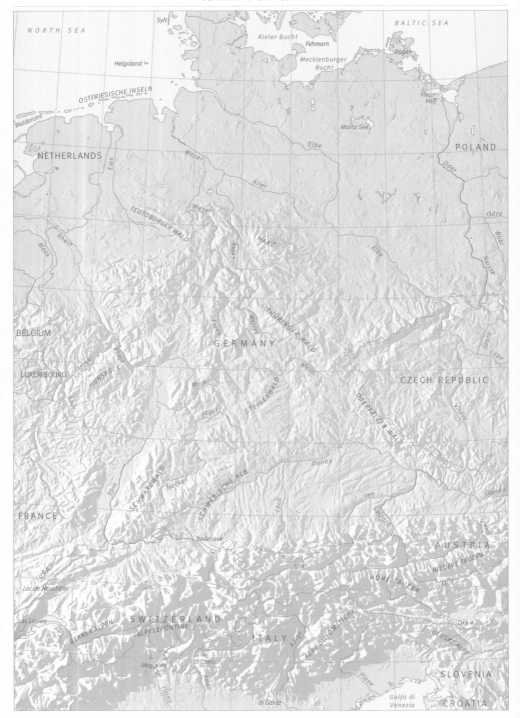

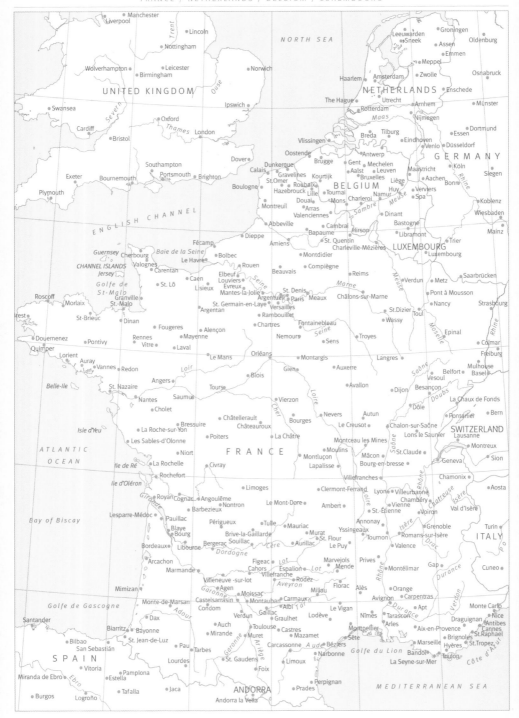

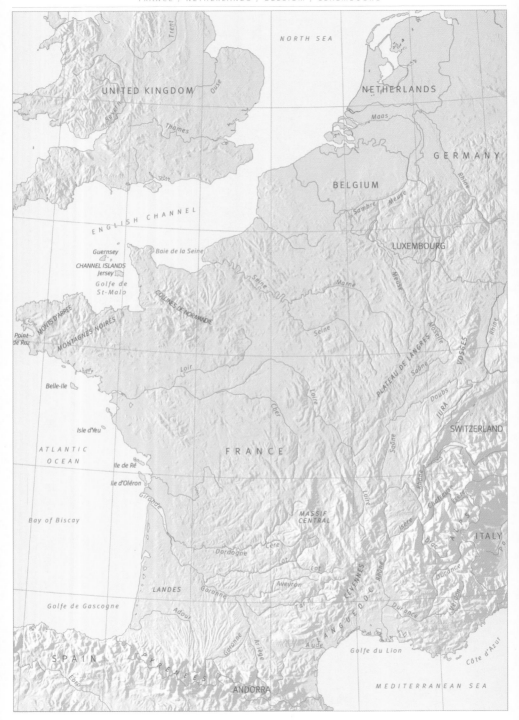

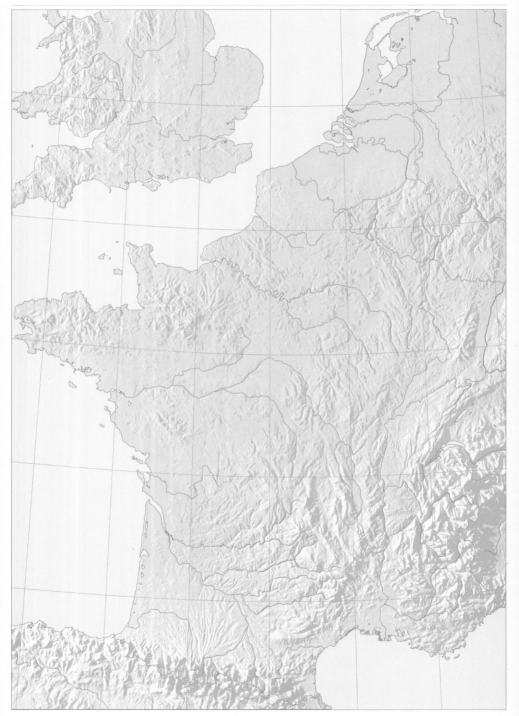

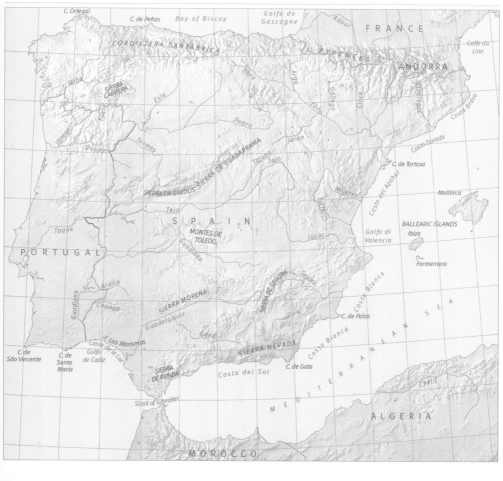

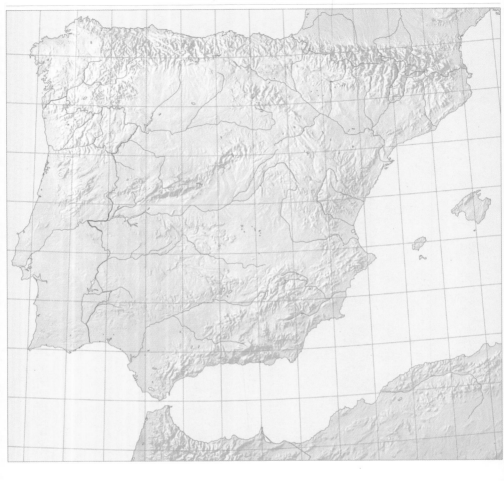

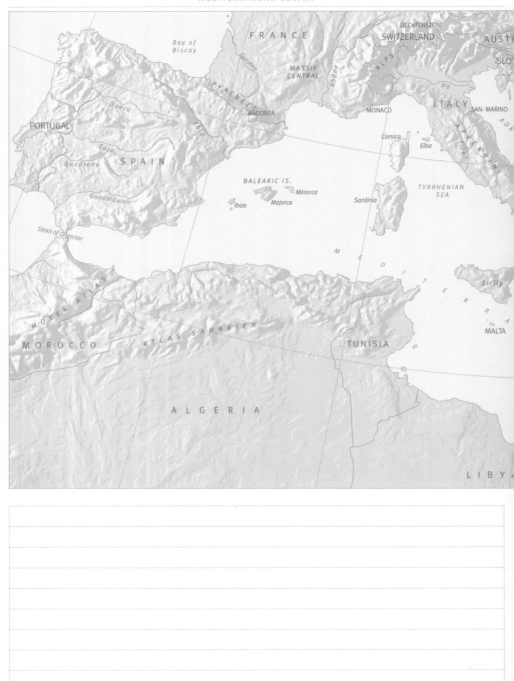

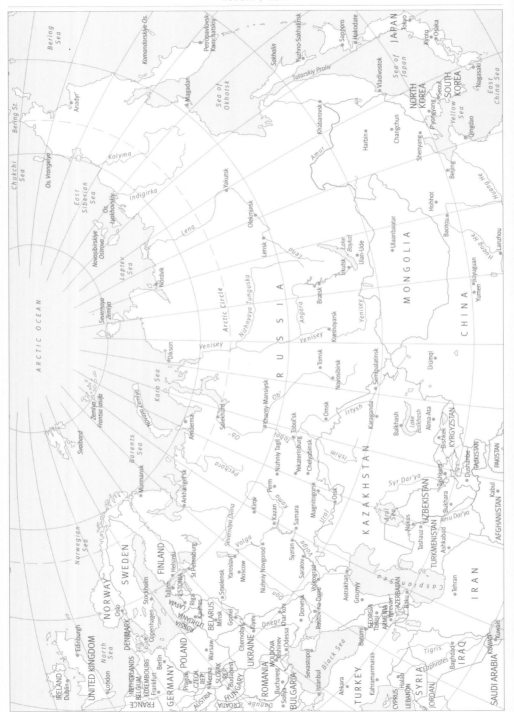

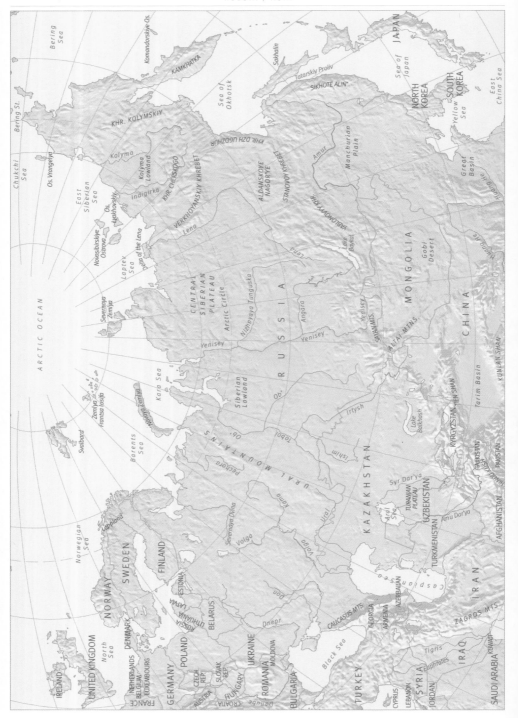

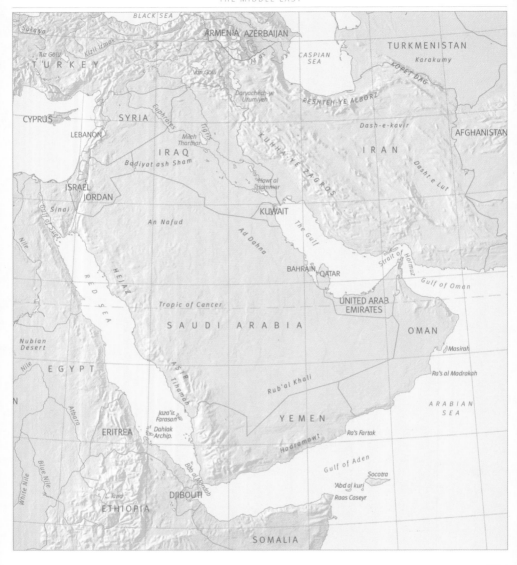

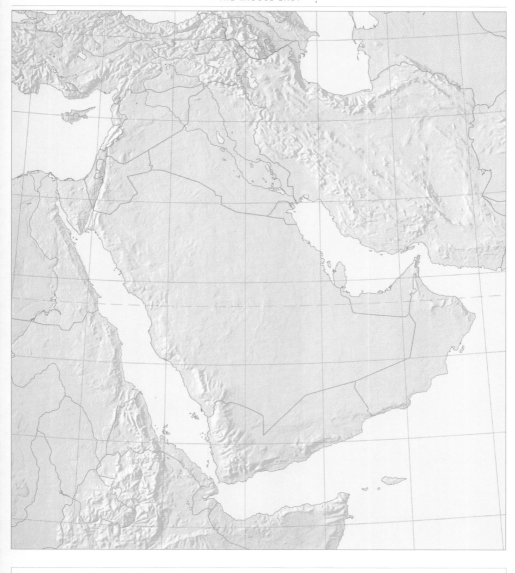

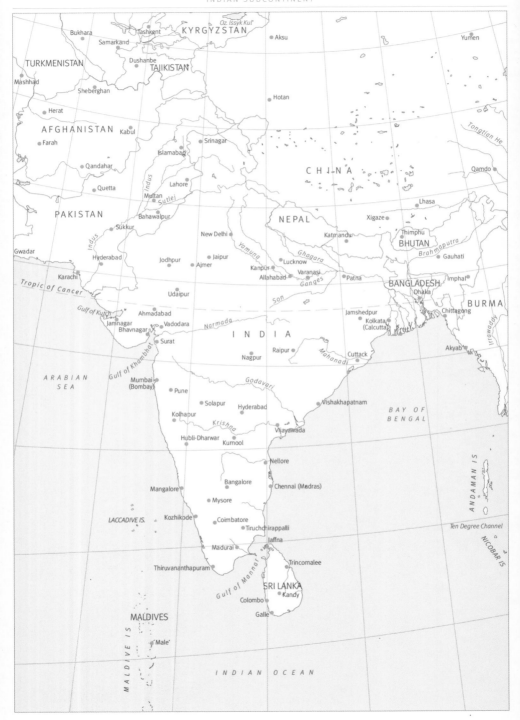

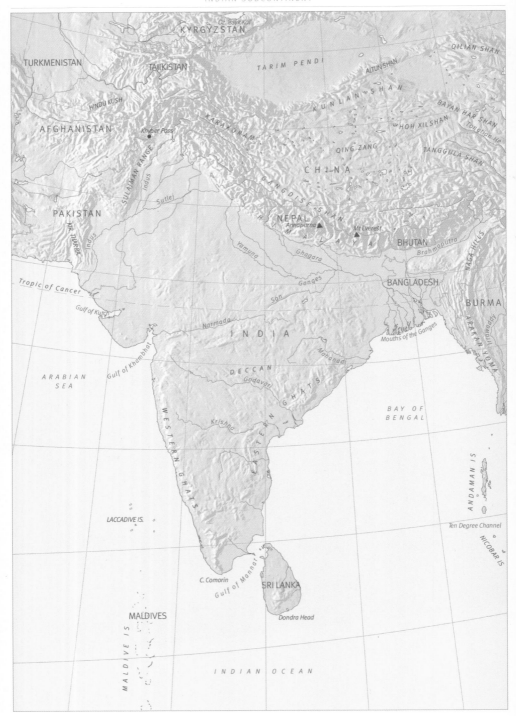

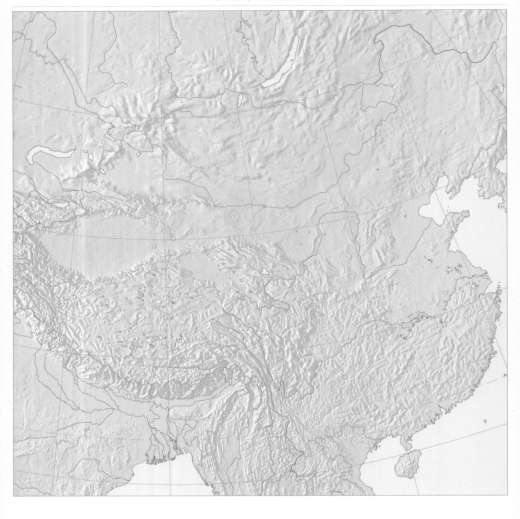

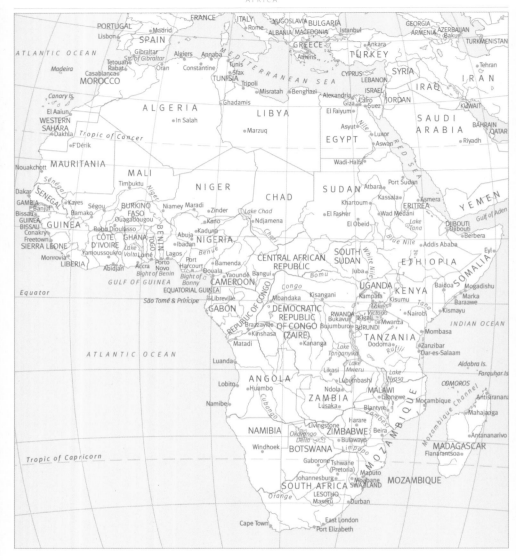

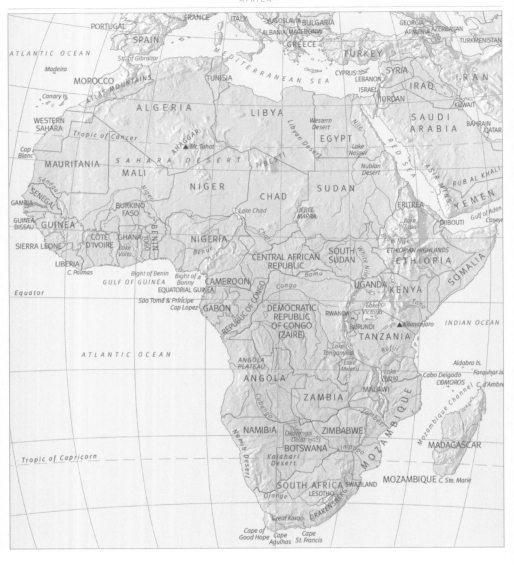

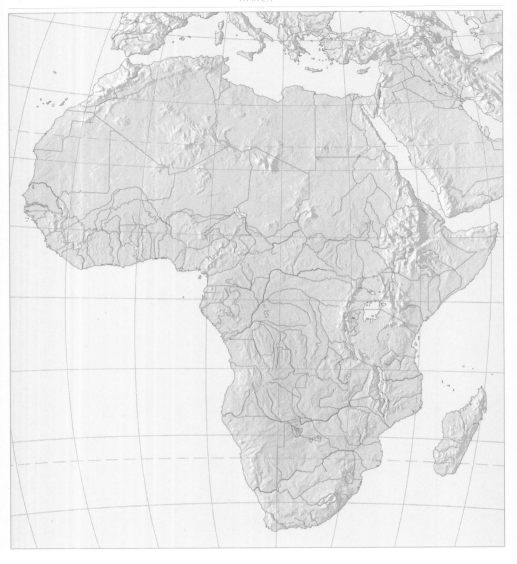

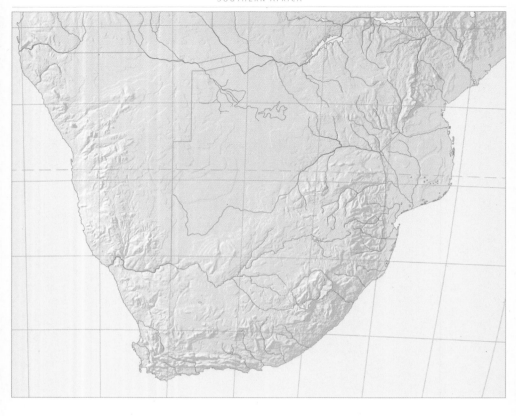

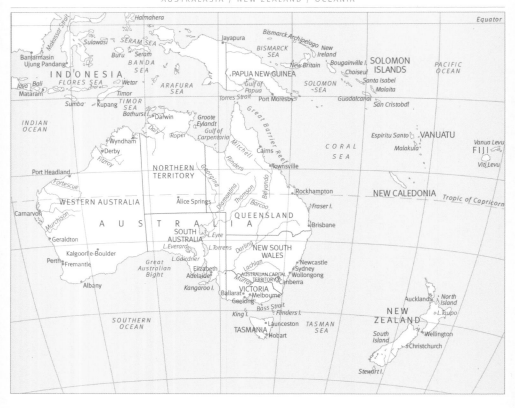

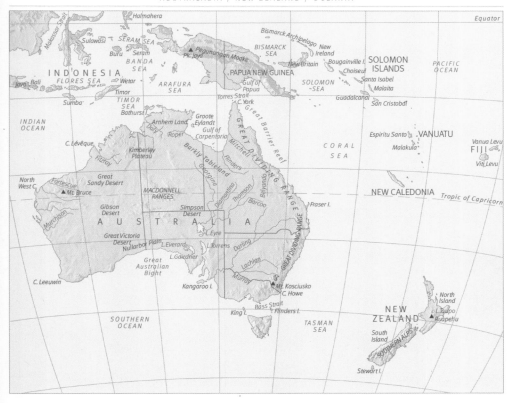

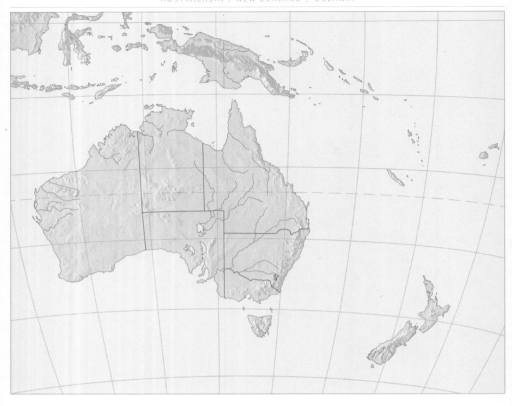

There are 15 types of electrical outlet plugs in use today (actually 16, but Type O is used exclusively in Thailand where it is rare), each of which has been assigned a letter by the U.S. Department of Commerce International Trade Administration (ITA). Although arbitrary, the system has been adopted worldwide to classify electrical outlets and plugs. The letter code is applied to both sockets and the plugs which fit them and is used in the travel data table on the following pages. Types A and C are the most commonly used electric plugs worldwide.

Bear in mind that many countries use a variety of plugs (often incompatible) and that the voltage may differ from region to region, making it hard to assess what kind of adapter or transformer you will need for your trip. Although appliances used in North America are designed to operate on 110-120 V (Volts), most of the world operates on 220-240 V. Thus, when traveling overseas, it's important that you check that your appliances' voltage requirements match the voltage in the country you are visiting. Failure to do so could severely damage or destroy your appliance, and could also be a fire risk. Fortunately, chargers that come with many modern gadgets such as smartphones use plugs or adapters that switch automatically between voltages in the 110–220 v range.

Socket Type A	**Socket Type B**
2 pins	3 pins
Not grounded/earthed	Grounded/earthed
Usually 100–127 V; 15 A	Usually 100–127 V; 15 A
Plug type A	Plug types A & B

Socket Type C	**Socket Type D**	**Socket Type E**	**Socket Type F**
2 pins	3 pins	2 pins	2 pins
Not grounded/earthed	Grounded/earthed	Grounded/earthed	Grounded/earthed
220–240 V; 2.5 A	220–240 V; 5 A	220–240 V; 16 A	220–240 V; 16 A
Plug type C	Plug types C & D	Plug types C, E & F	Plug types C, E & F
	(not safe with plug Types E & F)		

Socket Type G	**Socket Type H**	**Socket Type I**	**Socket Type J**
3 pins	3 pins	2/3 pins	3 pins
Grounded/earthed	Grounded/earthed	Not grounded/earthed (2 pins)	Grounded/earthed
220–240 V; 13 A	220–240 V; 16 amp	Grounded/earthed (3 pins)	220–240 V; 10 A
Plug type G	Plug types C & H	220–240 V; 10 A	Plug types C & J
	(not safe with plug types E & F)	Plug type I	

Socket Type K	**Socket Type L**	**Socket Type M**	**Socket Type N**
3 pins	3 pins	3 pins	3 pins
Grounded/earthed	Grounded/earthed	Grounded/earthed	Grounded/earthed
220–240 V; 16 A	220–240 V; 10 or 16 A	220–240 V; 15 A	220–240 V; 10 & 20 A
Plug types C & K	Plug types C & L (10 A version)	Plug type M	Plug types C & N
(not safe with plug types E & F)	or type L (16 A version)		

The languages listed on these pages are the official languages of each country, meaning that some are used only in commerce and for official purposes and may be spoken by only a small proportion of the population.

Thus some languages more common in everyday use may not be listed. The letters listed under "Socket type" refer to the illustrations on the page headed "International Power Outlets" at the beginning of this section.

Country	Official language(s)	Currency	Voltage	Socket type
AFRICA				
Algeria	Arabic, French	Dinar (100 centimes) (DZD)	230V	C,F
Angola	Portuguese	Kwanza (100 centimos) (AOA)	220V	C
Benin	French	West African CFA Franc (100 centimes) (XOF)	220V	C, E
Botswana	English; Setswana	Pula (100 Thebe) (BWP)	230V	D, G, M
Burkina Faso	French	West African CFA Franc (100 centimes) (XOF)	220V	C, E
Burundi	French; Kirundi	Burundi Franc (100 centimes) (BIF)	220V	C, E
Cameroon	French; English	Central African CFA Franc (100 centimes) (XAF)	220V	C, E
Cape Verde	Portuguese	Cape Verde Escudo (100 centavos) (CVE)	220V	C, F
Central African Republic	French	Central African CFA Franc (100 centimes) (XAF)	220V	C, E
Chad	French; Arabic	Central African CFA Franc (100 centimes) (XAF)	220V	C, D, E, F
Comoros	French; Arabic; Comorian	Comoros Franc (100 centimes) (KMF)	220V	C, E
Congo, Democratic Rep. of	French	Franc Congolais (100 centimes) (CDF)	230V	C, E
Congo, Republic of	French; Lingala	Central African CFA Franc (100 centimes) (XAF)	220V	C, D, E
Cote d'Ivoire	French	West African CFA Franc (100 centimes) (XOF)	230V	C, E
Djibouti	Arabic; French	Djibouti Franc (100 centimes) (DJF)	220V	C, E
Egypt	Arabic	Egyptian Pound (100 piastres) (EGP)	220V	C, F
Equatorial Guinea	Spanish; French	Central African CFA Franc (100 centimes) (XAF)	220V	C, E
Eritrea	Tigrinya; English; Arabic	Nakfa (100 cents) (ERN)	230V	C, L
Ethiopia	Amharic	Ethiopian Birr (100 cents) (ETB)	220V	C, E, F, L
Gabon	French	Central African CFA Franc (100 centimes) (XAF)	220V	C
Gambia	English	Gambian Dalasi (100 bututs) (GMD)	230V	G
Ghana	English	Ghana Cedi (100 Ghana pesewas) (GHS)	230V	D, G
Guinea	French	Guinea Franc (100 centimes) (GNF)	220V	C, F, K
Guinea-Bissau	Portuguese	West African CFA Franc (100 centimes) (XOF)	220V	C
Kenya	English; Kiswahili	Kenyan Shilling (100 cents) (KES)	240V	G
Lesotho	Sesotho; English	Loti (100 lisente) (LSL)	220V	M
Liberia	English	Liberian Dollar (100 cents) (LRD)	120/220V	A, B, C, E, F
Libya	Libyan Arabic	Libyan Dinar (1,000 dirhams) (LYD)	127/230V	C, D, F, L
Madagascar	Malagasy; French	Ariary (5 iraimbilanja) (MGA)	127/220V	C, D, E, J, K
Malawi	English; Chichewa	Kwacha (100 tambala) (MWK)	230V	G
Mali	French	West African CFA Franc (100 centimes) (XOF)	220V	C, E
Mauritania	Arabic	Mauritanian Ouguiya (5 khoums) (MRO)	220V	C
Mauritius	French; English	Mauritian Rupee (100 cents) (MUR)	230V	C, G
Morocco	Arabic	Moroccan Dirham (100 centimes) (MAD)	127/220V	C, E
Mozambique	Portuguese	Mozambique Metical (100 centavos) (MZN)	220V	C, F, M
Namibia	English	Namibian Dollar (100 cents) (NAD)	220V	D, M
Niger	French; Arabic	West African CFA Franc (100 centimes) (XOF)	220V	A, B, C, D, E, F
Nigeria	English	Naira (100 kobo) (NGN)	230V	D, G
Réunion	French	Euro (100 cents) (EUR)	220V	E
Rwanda	Kinyarwanda; French; English	Rwanda Franc (100 centimes) (RWF)	230V	C, J
São Tomé e Príncipe	Portuguese	Dobra (100 cêntimos) (STD)	220V	C, F
Senegal	French	West African CFA Franc (100 centimes) (XOF)	230V	C, D, E, K
Seychelles	Seychellois Creole; English; French	Seychelles Rupee (100 cents) (SCR)	240V	G
Sierra Leone	English	Leone (100 cents) (SLL)	230V	D, G

Currencies include the three-letter ISO 4217 code which is used by most currency conversion websites. Passport and visa advice on these pages apply only to nationals of Australia, Canada, the European Union, New Zealand, United Kingdom, and the United States. Nationals of all other countries are advised to contact the relevant embassies of countries they wish to visit for passport and visa requirements.

Passport	Visa	Notes
Yes	Yes	
Yes	Yes	
Yes	Yes	
Yes	No	
Yes	Yes	
Yes	Yes	
Yes	Yes	
Yes	Yes	
Yes	Yes	
Yes	Yes	
Yes	Yes	
Yes	Yes	
Yes	Yes	
Yes	Yes	
Yes	Yes	
Yes	Yes*	*Except EU and US nationals travelling to Sharm El Sheikh, Dahab, Nuweiba or Taba resorts for up to a maximum of 14 days, who do not need a visa and will receive an entry permission stamp on arrival.
Yes	Yes	
Yes	Yes	
Yes	Yes*	*Tourist visas can be issued on arrival at Addis Ababa Bole International Airport to foreign nationals coming from Australia, Austria, Belgium, Canada, Denmark, Finland, France, Germany, Greece, Ireland, Italy, Luxembourg, The Netherlands, Poland, Portugal, Spain, Sweden, the UK and the USA
Yes	Yes	
Yes	No*	*Except nationals of USA; Estonia; France; Portugal; Spain
Yes	Yes	
Yes	Yes	
Yes	Yes	
Yes	Yes*	*Except citizens of Cyprus
Yes	No*	*Except nationals of Bulgaria, Croatia, Cyprus, Estonia, Greece, Hungary, Latvia, Lithuania, Malta, Poland, Romania, Slovakia and Slovenia
Yes	Yes	
Yes	Yes	Visitors form all countries should seek advice from their government before traveling to Libya
Yes	Yes	
Yes	No*	*Except nationals of Austria, Bulgaria, Croatia, Czech Republic, Estonia, Greece, Hungary, Latvia, Lithuania, Poland, Romania, Slovakia and Slovenia, who require a visa
Yes	Yes	
Yes	Yes	
Yes	No	
Yes	No	
Yes	Yes	
Yes	No*	*Except nationals of Bulgaria, Croatia, Cyprus, Czech Republic, Estonia, Greece, Hungary, Latvia, Lithuania, Malta, Poland, Romania, Slovakia and Slovenia, who do require a visa
Yes	Yes	
Yes	Yes	
Yes*	No	*Passport or valid ID accepted for EU nationals
Yes	Yes*	*Except nationals of Germany, Sweden, the UK and the USA
Yes	Yes	
Yes	Yes	
Yes	No	
Yes	Yes	

Country	Official language(s)	Currency	Voltage	Socket type
Somalia	Somali; Arabic	100 cents = 1 Somali Shilling (SOS)	220V	C
South Africa	Afrikaans; English; IsiZulu; IsiXhosa	Rand (100 cents) (ZAR)	230V	C, D, M, N
South Sudan	English; Arabic	Sudanese Pound (100 piasters) (SDG)	230V	C, D
Sudan	Arabic; English	Sudanese Pound (100 piasters) (SDG)	230V	C, D
Swaziland	English; siSwati	Lilangeni (pl. Emalangeni) (100 cents) (SZL)	230V	M
Tanzania	Kiswahili (Swahili); English	Tanzanian Shilling (TZS)	230V	D, G
Togo	French	West African CFA Franc (100 centimes) (XOF)	220V	C
Tunisia	Arabic	Tunisian Dinar (1,000 millimes) (TND)	230V	C, E
Uganda	English	Uganda Shilling (UGX)	240V	G
Zambia	English	Zambian kwacha (100 ngwee) (ZMW)	230V	C, D, G
Zimbabwe	English	Multi-currency; US Dollar; S. African Rand	220V	D, G

ASIA				
Afghanistan	Pashto; Dari Persian	Afghani (100 puls) (AFN)	220V	C, F
Armenia	Armenian	Armenian Dram (100 luma) (AMD)	230V	C, F
Azerbaijan	Azeri	Azeri New Manat (100 gopik) (AZN)	220V	C, F
Bangladesh	Bengali (Bangla)	Bangladesh Taka (100 paisa) (BDT)	220V	C, D, G, K
Bhutan	Dzongkha	Ngultrum (100 chetrum) (BTN)	230V	C, D, F, G, M
Brunei	Malay	Brunei Dollar (100 cents) (BND)	240V	G
Cambodia	Khmer	Riel (KHR)	230V	A, C, G
China	Mandarin	Renminbi Yuan (10 jiao/mao or 100 fen) (CNY)	220V	A, C, I
East Timor: See Timor-Leste				
Georgia	Georgian	Lari (100 tetri) (GEL)	220V	C, F
Hong Kong	Cantonese; English	Hong Kong dollar (100 cents) (HKD)	220V	G, D
India	Hindi; English	Rupee (100 paise) (INR)	230V	C, D, M
Indonesia	Bahasa	Rupiah (IDR)	220/110V	C, F
Japan	Japanese	Yen (JPY)	100V	A, B
Kazakhstan	Kazakh	Kazakh Tenge (KZT)	220V	C, F
Kyrgyzstan	Kyrgyz	Kyrgyz Som (100 tyin) (KGS)	220V	C, F
Laos	Lao	Lao Kip (100 cents) (LAK)	230V	A, B, C, E, F
Macau	Cantonese; Portuguese	Pataca (100 avos) (MOP)	220V	D, M, G, F
Malaysia	Bahasa Melayu	Ringgit (100 sen) (MYR)	240V	A, C, G, M
Maldives	Dhivehi; English	Maldivian Rufiya (100 laari) (MVR)	230V	A, C, D, G, J, K, L
Mongolia	Khalkh Mongolian	Tugrik (MNT)	220V	C, E
Myanmar	Myanmar (Burmese)	Kyat (100 pyas) (MMK)	230V	C, D, F, G
Nepal	Nepali	Nepalese Rupee (100 paisa) (NPR)	230V	C, D, M
North Korea	Korean	Won (100 chon) (KPW)	220/110V	A, C, F
Pakistan	Urdu	Pakistan Rupee (PKR)	230V	C, D, G, M
Philippines	Filipino	Philippine Peso (100 centavos) (PHP)	220V	A, B, C
Singapore	Mandarin; English; Malay; Tamil	Singapore Dollar (100 cents) (SGD)	230V	C, G, M
South Korea	Korean (Hangul)	Won (KRW)	220V	C, F
Sri Lanka	Sinhala; Tamil	Sri Lanka Rupee (100 cents) (LKR)	230V	D, M, G
Taiwan	Mandarin Chinese	New Taiwan Dollar (100 cents) (TWD)	110V	A, B
Tajikistan	Tajik	Tajik Somoni (100 diram) (TJS)	220V	C, F, I
Thailand	Thai	Baht (100 satang) (THB)	220V	A, B, C, F
Timor-Leste (East Timor)	Tetum; Portuguese	US Dollar (100 cents) (USD)	220V	C, E, F, I
Turkmenistan	Turkmen	New Turkmenistan Manat (100 tenge) (TMT)	220V	A, B, C, E, F
Uzbekistan	Uzbek	Uzbek Som (100 tiyn) (UZS)	220V	C, I
Vietnam	Vietnamese	Dông (VND)	220V	A, C, F

CARIBBEAN				
Anguilla	English	East Caribbean Dollar (100 cents) (XCD)	110V	A

Passport	Visa	Notes
Yes	Yes	
Yes	No*	*Except nationals of Bulgaria, Croatia, Estonia, Lativa, Lithuania, Romania and Slovenia
Yes	Yes	
Yes	Yes	
Yes	No*	*Except nationals of Bulgaria and Romania
Yes	Yes*	*Except nationals of Cyprus and Romania, who do not require a visa
Yes	Yes	
Yes	No*	*Except nationals of Australia and Cyprus. Nationals of Czech Republic, Estonia, Latvia, Lithuania and Slovakia need a visa unless travelling as part of a package holiday
Yes	Yes	
Yes	Yes*	*Except nationals of Cyprus, Malta, Romania and Ireland, who do not require a visa unless travelling on business
Yes	Yes*	*Except nationals of Cyprus and Malta
Yes	Yes	Visitors form all countries should seek advice from their government before traveling to Afghanistan
Yes	Yes*	*EU nationals do not require a visa
Yes	Yes	
Yes	Yes	
Yes	Yes	
Yes	No*	*Except nationals of Croatia, who require a visa
Yes	Yes	
Yes	Yes*	*Unless visiting Hong Kong only
Yes*	No	*EU nationals may enter with national ID cards
Yes	No	
Yes	Yes	
Yes	Yes	
Yes	No	
Yes	Yes	
Yes	No*	*Except nationals of Bulgaria, Cyprus and Romania, who require a visa
Yes	Yes	
Yes	No	
Yes	No	
Yes	Yes	
Yes	Yes*	*Except US nationals travelling as tourists
Yes	Yes	
Yes	Yes	
Yes	Yes	Visitors form all countries should seek advice from their government before traveling to North Korea
Yes	Yes	
Yes	No*	*Except nationals of Croatia, who require a visa
Yes	No	
Yes	No	
Yes	Yes	
Yes	No*	*Except nationals of Croatia, who require a visa
Yes	Yes	
Yes	No*	*Except nationals of Bulgaria, Croatia, Cyprus, Estonia, Latvia, Lithuania, Malta and Romania, who require a visa
Yes	Yes*	*Except Portuguese nationals travelling as tourists, who do not require a visa
Yes	Yes	
Yes	Yes	
Yes	Yes*	*Except nationals of Denmark, Finland and Sweden
Yes	No	

Country	Official language(s)	Currency	Voltage	Socket type
Antigua and Barbuda	English	East Caribbean Dollar (100 cents) (XCD)	230V	A, B
Aruba	Dutch	Aruban Florin (100 cents) (AWG)	127V	A, B, F
Bahamas	English	Bahamian Dollar (100 cents) (BSD)	120V	A, B
Barbados	English	Barbados Dollar (100 cents) (BBD)	115V	A, B
Bermuda	English	Bermuda Dollar (100 cents) (BMD)	120V	A, B
Bonaire	Dutch	US Dollar (100 cents) (USD)	127/220V	A, B, C, F
British Virgin Islands	English	US Dollar (100 cents) (USD)	110V	A, B
Cayman Islands	English	Cayman Islands Dollar (100 cents) (KYD)	120V	A, B
Cuba	Spanish	Convertible Peso (100 centavos) (CUC)	110V	A, B
Curaçao: see Netherlands Antilles				
Dominica	English	East Caribbean Dollar (100 cents) (XCD)	230V	D, G
Dominican Republic	Spanish	Dominican Peso (DOP)	110V	A, B
Grenada	English	East Caribbean Dollar (100 cents) (XCD)	230V	G
Guadeloupe	French	Euro (100 cents) (EUR)	230V	C, D, E
Haiti	French; Creole	Gourde (100 centimes) (HTG)	110V	A, B
Jamaica	English	Jamaican Dollar (100 cents) (JMD)	110V	A, B
Martinique	French	Euro (100 cents) (EUR)	220V	C, D, E
Montserrat	English	East Caribbean Dollar (100 cents) (XCD)	230V	A, B
Netherlands Antilles	Dutch	Caribbean Guilder (100 cents) (CMG)	127/220V	A, B, C, F
Puerto Rico	Spanish; English	US Dollar (100 cents) (USD)	120V	A, B
Saba	Dutch	US Dollar (100 cents) (USD)	110V	A, B
Samoa	Samoan (Polynesian)	Tala or Samoa Dollar (100 sene) (WST)	230V	I
St Barthélemy	French	Euro (100 cents) (EUR)	220V	C, D
St Eustatius	Dutch	US Dollar (100 cents) (USD)	110V	A
St Kitts And Nevis	English	East Caribbean Dollar (100 cents) (XCD)	230V	A, B, D, G
St Lucia	English	East Caribbean Dollar (100 cents) (XCD)	240V	G
St Maarten: see Netherlands Antilles				
St Vincent and the Grenadines	English	East Caribbean Dollar (100 cents) (XCD)	230V	A, C, E, G, I, K
Trinidad and Tobago	English	Trinidad and Tobago Dollar (100 cents) (TTD)	115V	A, B
Turks and Caicos Islands	English	US Dollar (100 cents) (USD)	120V	A, B
US Virgin Islands	English	US Dollar (100 cents) (USD)	110V	A, B

EUROPE

Country	Official language(s)	Currency	Voltage	Socket type
Albania	Albanian	Lek (ALL)	230V	C, F
Andorra	Catalan	Euro (100 cents) (EUR)	230V	C,F
Austria	German; Croatian (in Burgenland)	Euro (100 cents) (EUR)	230V	C, F
Belarus	Belarusian; Russian	Belarusian Rouble (BYR)	220V	C, F
Belgium	Dutch; French; German	Euro (100 cents) (EUR)	230V	C, E
Bosnia and Herzegovina	Bosnian; Serbian; Croatian	Konvertibilna Marka (100 feninga) (BAM)	230V	C, F
Bulgaria	Bulgarian	Lev (100 stotinki) (BGN)	230V	C, F
Croatia	Croatian (Hrvatski)	Kuna (100 Lipa) (HRK)	230V	C, F
Cyprus	Greek; Turkish	Euro (100 cents) (EUR)	240V	G
Czech Republic	Czech	Korunaor or Crown (100 haler) (CZK)	230V	C, E
Denmark	Danish	Danish Krone (100 øre) (DKK)	230V	C, F, E, K
Estonia	Estonian	Euro (100 cents) (EUR)	230V	C, F
Finland	Finnish; Swedish	Euro (100 cents) (EUR)	230V	C, F
France	French	Euro (100 cents) (EUR)	230V	C, E
Germany	German	Euro (100 cents) (EUR)	230V	C, F
Gibraltar	English	Gibralter Pound (100 pence) (GBP)	240V	C, G
Greece	Greek	Euro (100 cents) (EUR)	230V	C, F
Hungary	Hungarian (Magyar)	Hungarian Forint (HUF)	230V	C, F
Iceland	Icelandic	Icelandic krona (100 aurar) (ISK)	230V	C, F
Ireland	Irish (Gaelic)	Euro (100 cents) (EUR)	230V	G

Passport	Visa	Notes
Yes	No*	*Except nationals of Croatia, who require a visa
Yes	No	
Yes	No	
Yes	No	
Yes	No	
Yes	No	
Yes*	No	*Canadian nationals can use an original birth certificate with valid photo ID
Yes*	No	*Canadian nationals can use an original birth certificate with valid photo ID unless travelling via USA
Yes	Yes	
Yes	No	
Yes	No*	*No visa, but tourist card required
Yes	No*	*Except nationals of Bulgaria and Croatia, who require a visa
Yes*	No	*Except EU nationals with a valid ID card
Yes	No	
Yes	No*	*Except nationals of Bulgaria, Croatia, Estonia, Hungary, Latvia, Lithuania, Romania and Slovenia, who require a visa
Yes*	No	*Except EU nationals with a valid ID card
Yes	No*	*Except nationals of Croatia, who require a visa
Yes	No	
Yes	No*	*Except nationals of Bulgaria, Croatia, Cyprus, Poland and Romania, who require a visa
Yes	No	
Yes	No	
Yes*	No	*Except EU nationals with a valid ID card
Yes	No	
Yes	No*	*Except nationals of Bulgaria and Croatia, who require a visa
Yes	No*	*Except nationals of Croatia, who require a visa
Yes	No	
Yes	No*	*Except nationals of Australia and South Africa, who require a visa
Yes*	No	*Canadian nationals can use an original birth certificate with valid photo ID
Yes	No*	*Except nationals of Bulgaria, Croatia, Cyprus, Poland and Romania, who require a visa
Yes*	No	*Passport or valid ID accepted for EU nationals
Yes*	No	*Passport or valid ID accepted for EU nationals
Yes*	No	*Passport or valid ID accepted for EU nationals
Yes	Yes	
Yes*	No	*Passport or valid ID accepted for EU nationals
Yes	No	
Yes*	No	*Passport or valid ID accepted for EU nationals
Yes*	No	*Passport or valid ID accepted for EU nationals
Yes*	No	*Passport or valid ID accepted for EU nationals
Yes*	No	*Passport or valid ID accepted for EU nationals
Yes*	No	*Passport or valid ID accepted for EU nationals
Yes*	No	*Passport or valid ID accepted for EU nationals
Yes*	No	*Passport or valid ID accepted for EU nationals
Yes*	No	*Passport or valid ID accepted for EU nationals
Yes*	No	*Passport or valid ID accepted for EU nationals
Yes*	No	*Passport or valid ID accepted for EU nationals
Yes*	No	*Passport or valid ID accepted for EU nationals
Yes*	No	*Passport or valid ID accepted for EU nationals
Yes*	No	*Passport or valid ID accepted for EU nationals
Yes*	No	*Passport or valid ID accepted for EU nationals
Yes*	No	*Except UK nationals travelling direct from the UK; Passport or valid ID accepted for EU nationals

Country	Official language(s)	Currency	Voltage	Socket type
Isle of Man	English	Manx Pound (100 pence) (IMP)	240V	C, G
Italy	Italian	Euro (100 cents) (EUR)	230V	C, F, L
Kosovo	Albanian; Serbian	Euro (100 cents) (EUR)	220V	C, E, F
Latvia	Latvian	Euro (100 cents) (EUR)	230V	C, F
Liechtenstein	German	Swiss Franc (100 centimes) (CHF)	230V	C, J
Lithuania	Lithuanian	Lithuanian Litas (100 centas) (LTL)	220V	C, F
Luxembourg	French; German; Lëtzeburgesch	Euro (100 cents) (EUR)	230V	C, F
Macedonia	Macedonian; Albanian	Macedonian Denar (100 deni) (MKD)	230V	C, F
Malta	Maltese; English	Euro (100 cents) (EUR)	230V	G
Moldova	Moldovan	Leu (100 bani) (MDL)	220V	C, F
Monaco	French	Euro (100 cents) (EUR)	230V	C, D, E, F
Montenegro	Montenegrin	Euro (100 cents) (EUR)	230V	C, F
Netherlands	Dutch	Euro (100 cents) (EUR)	230V	C, F
Norway	Norwegian (Bokmål; Nynorsk)	Norwegian Krone (100 øre) (NOK)	230V	C, F
Poland	Polish	Złoty (100 groszy) (PLN)	230V	C, E
Portugal	Portuguese; Mirandese	Euro (100 cents) (EUR)	230V	C, F
Romania	Romanian	New Leu (100 bani) (RON)	230V	C, F
Russia	Russian	Rouble (100 kopeks) (RUB)	220V	C, F
San Marino	Italian	Euro (100 cents) (EUR)	230V	C, F, L
Serbia	Serbian	Serbian Dinar (100 paras) (RSD)	230V	C, F
Slovakia	Slovak	Euro (100 cents) (EUR)	230V	C, E
Slovenia	Slovene	Euro (100 cents) (EUR)	230V	C, F
Spain	Spanish; Catalan (in Catalonia)	Euro (100 cents) (EUR)	230V	C, F
Sweden	Swedish	Swedish Krona (100 öre) (SEK)	230V	C, F
Switzerland	German; French; Italian; Romansch	Swiss Franc (100 cents) (CHF)	230V	C, J
Turkey	Turkish	New Turkish Lira (100 New Kurus) (TRY)	230V	C, F
Ukraine	Ukrainian	Hryvnya (100 kopiyok) (UAH)	220V	C, F
United Kingdom	English	Pound (100 pence) (GBP)	230V	G
Vatican City	Italian; Latin	Euro (100 cents) (EUR)	230V	C, F, L

MIDDLE EAST

Country	Official language(s)	Currency	Voltage	Socket type
Bahrain	Arabic	Dinar (1,000 fils) (BHD)	230V	G
Iran	Persian (Farsi)	Iranian Rial (100 dinars) (IRR)	220V	C, F
Iraq	Arabic; Kurdish	Iraqi Dinar (20 dirhams = 1,000 fils) (IQD)	230V	C, D, G
Israel	Hebrew; Arabic	New Shekel (100 agorot) (ILS)	230V	C, H, M
Jordan	Arabic	Dinar (100 piastres/qirsh or 1,000 fils) (JOD)	230V	B, C, D, F, G, J
Kuwait	Arabic	Kuwait Dinar (1,000 fils) (KWD)	240V	C, G
Lebanon	Arabic	Lebanese Pound (100 piastres) (LBP)	220V	A, B, C, D, G
Oman	Arabic	Omani Rial (1,000 baiza) (OMR)	240V	C, G
Palestinian National Authority	Arabic	New Shekel (100 agorot) (ILS)	220/230V	G, E
Qatar	Arabic	Qatari Riyal (100 dirhams) (QAR)	240V	D, G
Saudi Arabia	Arabic	Saudi Arabian Riyal (100 halala) (SAR)	127/220V	A, B, F, G
Syria	Arabic	Syrian Pound (100 piastres) (SYP)	220V	C, E, L
United Arab Emirates	Arabic	UAE Dirham (100 fils) (AED)	220V	C, D, G
Yemen	Arabic	Yemeni Riyal (100 fils) (YER)	230V	A, D, G

NORTH AMERICA

Country	Official language(s)	Currency	Voltage	Socket type
Belize	English	Belize Dollar (100 cents) (BZD)	110/220V	A, B, G
Canada	English; French	Canadian Dollar (100 cents) (CAD)	120V	A, B

Passport	Visa	Notes
Yes*	No	*Passport or valid ID accepted for EU nationals
Yes*	No	*Passport or valid ID accepted for EU nationals
Yes*	No	*Passport or valid ID accepted for EU nationals
Yes*	No	*Passport or valid ID accepted for EU nationals
Yes*	No	*Passport or valid ID accepted for EU nationals
Yes*	No	*Passport or valid ID accepted for EU nationals
Yes*	No	*Passport or valid ID accepted for EU nationals
Yes	No	
Yes*	No	*Passport or valid ID accepted for EU nationals
Yes	No	
Yes*	No	*Passport or valid ID accepted for EU nationals
Yes*	No	*Passport or valid ID accepted for EU nationals
Yes*	No	*Passport or valid ID accepted for EU nationals
Yes*	No	*Passport or valid ID accepted for EU nationals
Yes*	No	*Passport or valid ID accepted for EU nationals
Yes*	No	*Passport or valid ID accepted for EU nationals
Yes*	No	*Passport or valid ID accepted for EU nationals
Yes	Yes	
Yes*	No	*Passport or valid ID accepted for EU nationals
Yes*	No	*Passport or valid ID accepted for EU nationals
Yes*	No	*Passport or valid ID accepted for EU nationals
Yes*	No	*Passport or valid ID accepted for EU nationals
Yes*	No	*Passport or valid ID accepted for EU nationals
Yes*	No	*Passport or valid ID accepted for EU nationals
Yes*	No	*Passport or valid ID accepted for EU nationals
Yes	Yes*	*Except nationals of Bulgaria, Czech Republic, Denmark, Estonia, Finland, France, Germany, Greece, Italy, Lithuania, Luxembourg, Romania, Slovakia, Slovenia and Sweden
Yes	No*	*Except nationals of Australia, who require a visa
Yes*	No	*Passport or valid ID accepted for EU nationals
Yes*	No	*Passport or valid ID accepted for EU nationals
Yes	Yes*	*Available at the airport for nationals of Australia, Austria, Belgium, Canada, Cyprus, Denmark, Finland, France, Germany, Greece, Hungary, Ireland, Italy, Luxembourg, the Netherlands, Portugal, Spain, Sweden, Switzerland, UK and USA
Yes	Yes	
Yes	Yes	Visitors form all countries should seek advice from their government before traveling to Iraq
Yes	No	
Yes	Yes	
Yes	Yes	
Yes	Yes	
Yes	Yes	
Yes	No	
Yes	Yes	
Yes	Yes	
Yes	Yes	Visitors form all countries should seek advice from their government before traveling to Syria
Yes	Yes	
Yes	Yes	
Yes	No	
Yes*	No**	*Except citizens of the USA holding a birth certificate, certificate of citizenship or naturalisation, US permanent resident card, or certificate of Indian status along with photo ID. However, it is recommended that you carry a valid passport. US citizens re-entering the USA from Canada via air, land or sea will require a valid passport or passport card. **Except Nationals of Bulgaria and Romania.

Country	Official language(s)	Currency	Voltage	Socket type
Costa Rica	Spanish	Costa Rican Colón (100 céntimos) (CRC)	120V	A, B
El Salvador	Spanish	US Dollar (100 cents) (USD)	115V	A, B
Greenland	Greenlandic (East Inuit); Danish	Danish Krone (100 øre) (DKK)	230V	C, F, E, K
Guatemala	Spanish	Quetzal (GTQ)	120V	A, B
Honduras	Spanish	Lempira (100 centavos) (HNL)	110V	A, B
Mexico	Spanish	Mexican Peso (100 centavos) (MXN)	127V	A, B
Nicaragua	Spanish	Nicaraguan Gold Córdoba (100 centavos) (NIO)	120V	A, B
Panama	Spanish	Balboa (100 centésimos) (PAB); US Dollar	110V	A, B
United States of America	English (28 States); Hawaiian (in Hawaii)	US Dollar (100 cents) (USD)	120V	A, B

OCEANIA

Country	Official language(s)	Currency	Voltage	Socket type
American Samoa	Samoan	US Dollar (100 cents) (USD)	120V	A, B, F, I
Australia	English	Australian Dollar (100 cents) (AUD)	230V	I
Cook Islands	English; Cook Islands Maori (Rarotongan)	New Zealand Dollar (100 cents) (NZD)	240V	I
Fiji	English; Fijian	Fijian Dollar (100 cents) (FJD)	240V	I
French Polynesia	French; Polynesian	French Pacific Franc (100 centimes) (XPF)	110/220V	A, C
Guam	English	US Dollar (100 cents) (USD)	110V	A, B
Kiribati	I-Kiribati; English	Australian Dollar (100 cents) (AUD)	240V	I
Marshall Islands	Marshallese; English	US Dollar (100 cents) (USD)	120V	A, B
Micronesia, Federated States of	English	US Dollar (100 cents) (USD)	120V	A, B
Nauru	Nauruan	Australian Dollar (100 cents) (AUD)	240V	I
New Caledonia	French	French Pacific Franc (CPF)	220V	C, F
New Zealand	English; Maori	New Zealand Dollar (100 cents) (NZD)	230V	I
Niue	Niuean; English	New Zealand Dollar (100 cents) (NZD)	240V	I
Northern Mariana Islands	Chamorro; English	US Dollar (100 cents) (USD)	120V	A, B
Palau	Palauan; English	US Dollar (100 cents) (USD)	120V	A, B
Papua New Guinea	Tok Pisin; English; Hiri Motu	Kina (100 toea) (PGK)	240V	I
Solomon Islands	English	Solomon Islands Dollar (100 cents) (SBD)	220V	I, G
Tonga	Tongan; English	Pa'anga (100 seniti) (TOP)	240V	I
Tuvalu	Tuvaluan; English	Tuvaluan Dollar (100 cents) (TVD)*	220V	I
Vanuatu	Bislama (creole); English; French	Vatu (100 centimes) (VUV)	220V	C, G, I

SOUTH AMERICA

Country	Official language(s)	Currency	Voltage	Socket type
Argentina	Spanish	Peso (100 centavos) (ARS)	220V	C, I
Bolivia	Spanish; Quechua; Aymara; Guarani	Bolivianos or pesos (100 centavos) (BOB)	115/230V	A, C
Brazil	Portuguese	Real/Reais (100 centavos) (BRL)	127/220V	C, N
Chile	Spanish	Chilean Peso (100 centavos) (CLP)	220V	C, L
Colombia	Spanish	Colombian Peso (100 centavos) (COP)	110V	A, B
Ecuador	Spanish	US Dollar (100 cents) (USD)	120V	A, B
Falkland Is. (Islas Malvinas)	English	Falkland Islands Pound (FKP); UK Pound (GBP)	240V	G
French Guiana	French	Euro (100 cents) (EUR)	220V	C, D, E
Guyana	English	Guyanese Dollar (100 cents) (GYD)	240V	A, B, D, G
Paraguay	Spanish; Guarani	Guaraní (PYG)	220V	C
Peru	Spanish; Quechua; Aymara	Nuevo Sol (100 céntimos) (PEN)	220V	A, B, C
Suriname	Dutch	Surinam Dollar (100 cents) (SRD)	127V	C, F
Uruguay	Spanish	Peso Uruguayo (100 centécimos) (UYU)	230V	C, F, I, L
Venezuela	Spanish	Bolívar Fuerte (100 céntimos) (VEF)	120V	A, B

Passport	Visa	Notes
Yes	No	
Yes	No*	*Except nationals of Australia, Bulgaria, Croatia, Latvia and Romania, who must purchase a tourist card on entry
Yes*	No	*Passport or valid ID accepted for EU nationals
Yes	No	
Yes	No	
Yes	No	
Yes	No	
Yes	No	
Yes	No	*Except nationals of Bulgaria, Croatia, Cyprus, Poland and Romania, who are not included in the Visa Waiver Program so require a visa
Yes	No	
Yes	Yes	
Yes	No	
Yes	No*	*Except nationals of Croatia and Lithuania, who need a visa
Yes	No	
Yes*	No**	*US citizens may be able to enter Guam from the US mainland or a US territory with proof of citizenship and a valid photo ID card, but a passport is advised **Nationals of Bulgaria, Croatia, Cyprus, Poland and Romania should check the USA passport & visa section for visa requirements
Yes	No	
Yes	Yes*	*Except nationals of the USA
Yes	No	
Yes	Yes	
Yes	No	
Yes	No	
Yes	No	
Yes	No*	*Except nationals of Bulgaria, Croatia, Cyprus, Poland and Romania, who require a visa
Yes	No	
Yes	Yes	
Yes	No	
Yes	No*	*Except nationals of Croatia, who require a visa
Yes	No	*Transactions over A$1 are always conducted in Australian Dollars
Yes	No	
Yes	No*	*Except nationals of Canadian, Austria, Cyprus, Germany, Greece, Italy, Luxembourg, Malta, Portugal, Slovakia and Spain travelling for business purposes only, who require a visa
Yes	No*	*Except nationals of Bulgaria, Cyprus, Malta, and Romania, who require a visa
Yes	Yes*	*Except nationals of all EU countries
Yes	No*	*Nationals of Australia and Canada must pay a reciprocal tax at point of entry.
Yes	No*	*Except nationals of Bulgaria, who require a visa
Yes	No	
Yes	No	
Yes*	No	*Except nationals of France who hold national identity cards
Yes	No*	*Except nationals of Bulgaria, Croatia, Cyprus, the Czech Republic, Estonia, Hungary, Latvia, Lithuania, Malta, Poland, Romania, Slovakia and Slovenia, who require a visa
Yes	Yes*	*Except nationals of all EU countries
Yes	No	
Yes	Yes	
Yes	No	
Yes	No	

Greenwich Mean Time (GMT) was adopted as the world's time standard at the Washington Meridian Conference in 1884. Universal Time was also established, from which the international 24-hour time-zone system grew. Although the prime meridian at Greenwich, in the United Kingdom, served as the reference line for GMT, worldwide standard for coordinated universal time is now abbreviated as UTC (sometimes referred to as UTC/GMT). The current UTC time zones are shown on this world map, the starting time zone, or 0, being located either side of the Greenwich meridian. UTC is also used in

aviation and is informally known as Zulu Time to avoid confusion about time zones and daylight saving time—"Zulu" being the letter code for 0 in the International Radiotelephony Spelling Alphabet. These letter codes, known as the NATO phonetic alphabet, are also used by the military and are shown on the map below. Daylight saving time (DST, or summer time)—observed by some countries— is not shown on the map below, and all times are based directly on UTC. Although the UK observes DST (called British Summer Time, or BST), UTC time in Greenwich, England, does not.

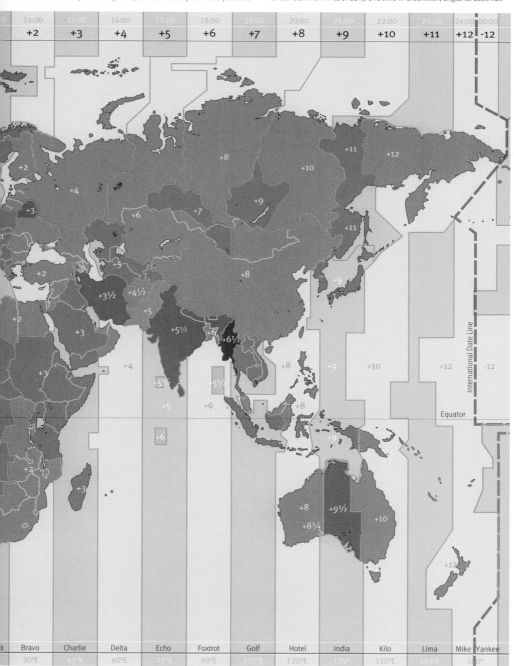

	14:00	15:00	16:00	17:00	18:00	19:00	20:00	21:00	22:00	23:00	24:00	00:00
	+2	+3	+4	+5	+6	+7	+8	+9	+10	+11	+12	-12

International Date Line

Equator

a	Bravo	Charlie	Delta	Echo	Foxtrot	Golf	Hotel	India	Kilo	Lima	Mike	Yankee
	30°E	45°E	60°E	75°E	90°E	105°E	120°E	135°E	150°E	165°E	180°	

DISTANCE TABLE

This table shows distances between a selection of major cities around the world. Distances are in miles, in black, in the lower left portion of the table, and kilometres, in red, in the upper right portion, the distance calculated by either selecting a city from the list across the top of the table or from down the left hand side. Distances are straight line distances, known as "great circle distance", being the shortest route between two locations

Distances in miles / Distances in kilometres	Beijing	Berlin	Buenos Aires	Cairo	Kolkata	Cape Town	Caracas	Chicago	Hong Kong	Honolulu	Istanbul	Johannesburg	Lisbon	London
Beijing	—	7,353	19,258	7,538	3,253	12,941	14,394	10,601	1,973	8,157	7,049	11,700	9,662	8,136
Berlin	4,570	—	11,910	2,888	7,028	9,623	8,442	7,088	8,753	11,760	1,735	8,866	2,311	932
Buenos Aires	11,969	7,402	—	11,818	16,516	6,869	5,097	9,007	18,458	12,166	12,246	8,093	9,583	11,128
Cairo	4,685	1,795	7,345	—	5,694	7,241	10,198	9,862	8,143	14,220	1,236	6,262	3,802	3,509
Kolkata	2,022	4,368	10,265	3,539	—	9,693	15,454	12,840	2,652	11,339	5,854	8,465	9,072	7,960
Cape Town	8,043	5,981	4,269	4,500	6,024	—	10,241	13,667	11,866	18,558	8,293	1,255	8,568	9,673
Caracas	8,946	5,247	3,168	6,338	9,605	6,365	—	4,024	16,359	9,675	9,731	11,012	6,502	7,498
Chicago	6,589	4,405	5,598	6,129	7,980	8,494	2,501	—	12,539	6,838	8,812	13,984	6,420	6,356
Hong Kong	1,226	5,440	11,472	5,061	1,648	7,375	10,167	7,793	—	8,928	8,019	10,689	11,026	9,625
Honolulu	5,069	7,309	7,561	8,838	7,047	11,534	6,013	4,250	5,549	—	13,047	19,197	12,582	11,630
Istanbul	4,381	1,078	7,611	768	3,638	5,154	6,048	5,477	4,984	8,109	—	7,472	3,237	2,497
Johannesburg	7,272	5,510	5,030	3,892	5,261	780	6,844	8,691	6,643	11,931	4,644	—	8,188	9,071
Lisbon	6,005	1,436	5,956	2,363	5,638	5,325	4,041	3,990	6,853	7,820	2,012	5,089	—	1,585
London	5,056	579	6,916	2,181	4,947	6,012	4,660	3,950	5,982	7,228	1,552	5,637	985	—
Los Angeles	6,251	5,724	6,170	7,520	8,090	9,992	3,632	1,745	7,195	2,574	6,783	10,373	5,621	5,382
Madrid	5,734	1,166	6,236	2,086	5,331	5,330	4,341	4,178	6,542	7,860	1,705	5,036	307	789
Manila	1,772	6,132	11,051	5,704	2,203	7,486	10,620	8,143	693	5,299	5,664	6,835	7,546	6,672
Mexico City	7,740	6,047	4,592	7,688	9,492	8,517	2,232	1,691	8,782	3,779	7,110	9,065	5,390	5,550
Montreal	6,500	3,729	5,615	5,414	7,607	7,931	2,449	744	7,729	4,910	4,789	8,034	3,246	3,282
Moscow	3,594	1,004	8,376	1,803	3,321	6,300	6,173	4,974	4,439	7,037	1,091	5,668	2,427	1,555
New York	6,826	3,965	5,297	5,602	7,918	7,764	2,132	713	8,054	4,964	4,975	7,980	3,364	3,458
Paris	5,104	545	6,870	1,995	4,883	5,807	4,736	4,134	5,985	7,438	1,400	5,425	904	213
Rio de Janeiro	10,762	6,220	1,200	6,146	9,377	3,773	2,810	5,296	11,021	8,285	6,389	4,428	4,796	5,766
Rome	5,047	734	6,929	1,320	4,482	5,249	5,196	4,808	5,768	8,022	843	4,809	1,161	887
San Francisco	5,914	5,661	6,467	7,364	7,814	10,247	3,904	1,858	6,897	2,393	6,703	10,543	5,666	5,357
Shanghai	665	5,218	12,201	5,183	2,117	8,061	9,501	7,061	764	4,941	4,962	7,317	6,654	5,715
Stockholm	4,166	504	7,808	2,111	4,195	6,444	5,420	4,278	5,113	6,862	1,348	5,937	1,856	890
Sydney	5,562	10,006	7,330	8,952	5,685	6,843	9,513	9,272	4,584	4,943	9,294	6,859	11,302	10,564
Tokyo	1,305	5,540	11,408	5,935	3,194	9,156	8,799	6,299	1,794	3,853	5,560	8,414	6,915	5,940
Warsaw	4,311	320	7,662	1,630	4,048	5,958	5,517	4,667	5,144	7,355	863	5,437	1,715	899
Washington, D.C.	6,925	4,169	5,218	5,800	8,084	7,901	2,059	597	8,147	4,519	5,215	8,130	3,562	3,663

Centered on Beijing

Centered on Buenos Aires

Centered on Cairo

Centered on Kolkata

Centered on Cape Town

Centered on Caracas

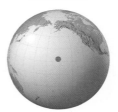

Centered on Honolulu

Centered on Istanbul

on a sphere. This distance may be different from the actual travel distance.
The globe views on these pages show a selection of the cities below
displayed as center points on the globe.

Los Angeles	Madrid	Manila	Mexico City	Montreal	Moscow	New York	Paris	Rio de Janeiro	Rome	San Francisco	Shanghai	Stockholm	Sydney	Tokyo	Warsaw	Washington, D.C.
10,058	9,225	2,851	12,453	10,459	5,784	10,983	8,212	17,315	8,121	9,515	1,070	6,704	8,949	2,099	6,936	11,142
9,210	1,876	9,866	9,730	6,000	1,615	6,380	877	10,008	1,181	9,109	8,396	811	16,100	8,914	515	6,708
9,928	10,034	17,781	7,389	9,035	13,477	8,523	11,054	1,931	11,149	10,405	19,631	12,563	11,794	18,355	12,328	8,396
12,100	3,356	9,178	12,370	8,711	2,901	9,014	3,210	9,889	2,124	11,849	8,339	3,397	14,404	9,549	2,623	9,332
13,017	8,578	3,545	15,273	12,240	5,343	12,740	7,857	15,088	7,212	12,573	3,406	6,750	9,147	5,139	6,513	13,007
16,077	8,576	12,045	13,704	12,761	10,137	12,492	9,343	6,071	8,446	16,487	12,970	10,368	11,010	14,732	9,586	12,713
5,844	6,985	17,088	3,591	3,940	9,932	3,430	7,620	4,521	8,360	6,282	15,287	8,721	15,306	14,158	8,877	3,313
2,808	6,722	13,102	2,721	1,197	8,003	1,147	6,652	8,521	7,736	2,990	11,361	6,883	14,919	10,135	7,509	961
11,577	10,526	1,115	14,130	12,436	7,142	12,959	9,630	17,733	9,281	11,097	1,229	8,227	7,376	2,887	8,277	13,109
4,142	12,647	8,526	6,080	7,900	11,323	7,987	11,968	13,331	12,907	3,850	7,950	11,041	7,953	6,199	11,834	7,271
10,914	2,743	9,113	11,440	7,706	1,755	8,005	2,253	10,280	1,356	10,785	7,984	2,169	14,954	8,946	1,389	8,391
16,690	8,103	10,998	14,585	12,927	9,120	12,839	8,728	7,125	7,738	16,964	11,773	9,553	11,035	13,538	8,748	13,081
9,044	494	12,142	8,673	5,223	3,905	5,413	1,455	7,717	1,868	9,117	10,706	2,986	18,185	11,126	2,759	5,731
8,660	1,270	10,735	8,930	5,281	2,502	5,564	343	9,277	1,427	8,619	9,195	1,432	16,997	9,557	1,446	5,894
—	9,358	11,683	2,557	3,905	9,659	3,944	8,991	10,187	10,832	558	10,359	8,775	12,116	8,742	9,528	3,701
5,816	—	11,661	9,056	5,532	3,458	5,762	1,060	8,130	1,371	9,325	10,261	2,600	17,687	10,770	2,298	6,113
7,261	7,247	—	14,216	13,171	8,256	13,673	10,743	18,116	10,389	11,210	1,850	9,327	6,346	3,002	9,392	13,776
1,589	5,628	8,835	—	3,730	10,721	3,369	9,197	7,677	10,243	3,036	12,907	9,588	12,956	11,297	10,241	3,036
2,427	3,438	8,186	2,318	—	7,057	515	5,506	8,201	6,565	4,085	11,348	5,900	16,016	10,270	6,450	785
6,003	2,149	5,131	6,663	4,386	—	7,506	2,484	11,545	2,372	9,446	6,814	1,226	14,500	7,477	1,150	7,817
2,451	3,581	8,498	2,094	320	4,665	—	5,831	7,751	6,888	4,137	11,860	6,314	15,982	10,845	6,989	330
5,588	659	6,677	5,716	3,422	1,544	3,624	—	9,170	1,121	8,943	9,258	1,541	16,965	9,709	1,366	6,161
6,331	5,053	11,259	4,771	5,097	7,175	4,817	5,699	—	9,146	10,653	18,240	10,701	13,364	18,557	10,405	7,717
6,732	852	6,457	6,366	4,080	1,474	4,281	697	5,684	—	10,040	9,134	1,986	16,309	9,871	1,315	7,134
347	5,795	6,967	1,887	2,539	5,871	2,571	5,558	6,621	6,240	—	9,879	8,626	11,932	8,262	9,398	3,929
6,438	6,377	1,150	8,022	7,053	4,235	7,371	5,754	11,336	5,677	6,140	—	7,763	7,882	1,765	7,966	11,984
5,454	1,616	5,797	5,959	3,667	762	3,924	958	6,651	1,234	5,361	4,825	—	15,601	8,127	806	6,634
7,530	10,993	3,944	8,052	9,954	9,012	9,933	10,544	8,306	10,136	7,416	4,899	9,696	—	7,829	15,601	15,701
5,433	6,694	1,866	7,021	6,383	4,647	6,740	6,034	11,533	6,135	5,135	1,097	5,051	4,866	—	8,446	10,896
5,922	1,428	5,837	6,365	4,009	715	4,344	849	6,467	817	5,841	4,951	501	9,696	5,249	—	7,171
2,300	3,799	8,562	1,887	488	4,858	205	3,829	4,796	4,434	2,442	7,448	4,123	9,758	6,772	4,457	—

Centered on London

Centered on Los Angeles

Centered on Manila

Centered on Moscow

Centered on New York

Centered on Rio de Janeiro

Centered on Sydney

Centered on Tokyo

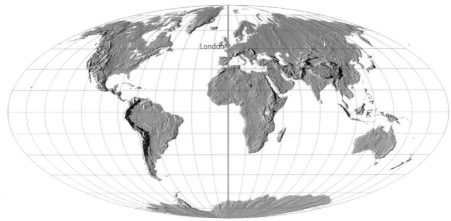

Longitude centered on London (0°)

Longitude centered on Los Angeles (118° W)

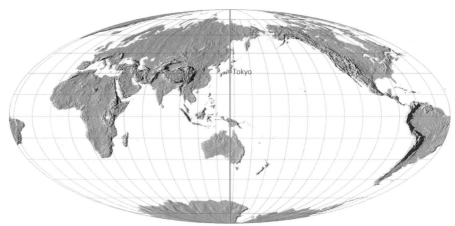

Longitude centered on Tokyo (139° E)

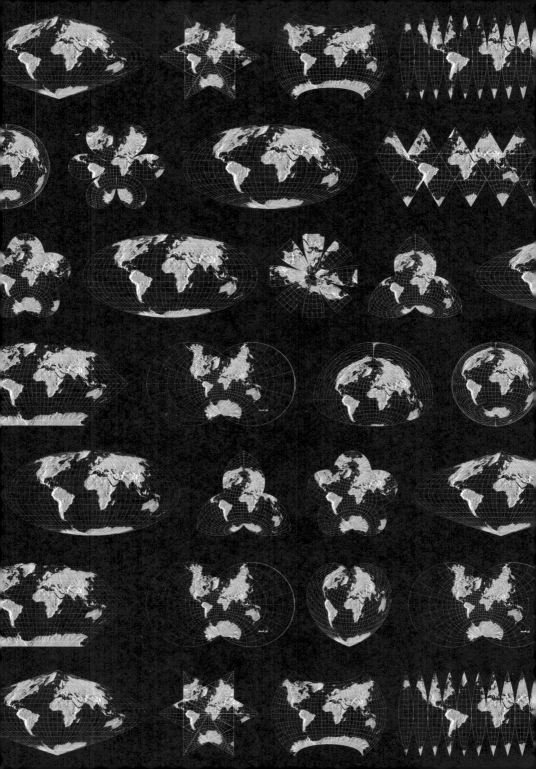